YOU'RE THE CHEF

TASTY Sandwiches

Jennifer S. Larson Photographs by **Brie Cohen**

M MILLBROOK PRESS • MINNEAPOLIS

For Eleanor and Katie—J.S.L.

For my dad, who can make one heck of a grilled cheese sandwich—B.C.

Photography by Brie Cohen
Food in photographs prepared by chef David Vlach
Illustrations by Laura Westlund/Independent Picture Service
The image on page 5 is used with the permission of © iStockphoto.com/stuartbur.

Allergy alert: The recipes in this book contain ingredients to which some people can be allergic. Anyone with food allergies or sensitivities should follow the advice of a physician or other medical professional.

Millbrook Press
A division of Lerner Publishing Group, Inc.
241 First Avenue North
Minneapolis, MN 55401 U.S.A.

Website address: www.lernerbooks.com

Main body text set in Felbridge Standard.
Typeface provided by Monotype Typography.

Library of Congress Cataloging-in-Publication Data

Larson, Jennifer S., 1967– author.
Tasty sandwiches / by Jennifer S. Larson ;
photographs by Brie Cohen.
pages   cm — (You're the chef)
Includes index.
ISBN 978–0–7613–6643–0 (lib. bdg. : alk. paper)
1. Sandwiches—Juvenile literature. I. Cohen, Brie, illustrator. II. Title.
TX818.L37 2013
641.84—dc23   2012022478

Manufactured in the United States of America
1 – BP – 12/31/12

TABLE OF CONTENTS

Let's make some super sandwiches! YOU can be the chef and make food for yourself and your family. These easy recipes are perfect for a chef who is just learning to cook. And they're so delicious, you'll want to make them again and again!

I developed these recipes with the help of my kids, who are seven and ten years old. They can't do all the cooking on their own yet, but they can do a lot.

Can't get enough of cooking? Check out www.lerneresource.com for bonus recipes, healthful eating tips, links to cooking technique videos, metric conversions, and more!

BEFORE YOU START

Reserve your space! Always ask for permission to work in the kitchen.

Find a helper! You will need an adult helper for some tasks.

Make a plan! Read through the whole recipe before you start cooking. Do you have the ingredients you'll need? If you don't know what an ingredient is, see page 31 to find out more. Do you understand each step? If you don't understand a technique, such as *beat* or *slice*, turn to page 7. At the beginning of each recipe, you'll see how much time you'll need to prepare the recipe and to cook it. The recipe will also tell you how many servings it makes. Small drawings at the top of each recipe let you know what major kitchen equipment you'll need— such as a stovetop, a toaster, or a microwave.

stovetop

toaster

knives

microwave

oven

Wash up! Always wash your hands with soap and water before you start cooking. And wash them again after you touch raw eggs, meat, or fish.

Get it together! Find the tools you'll use, such as measuring cups or a mixing bowl. Gather all the ingredients you'll need. That way you won't have to stop to look for things once you start cooking.

SAFETY TIPS

That's sharp! Your adult helper needs to be in the kitchen when you are using a knife, a grater, or a vegetable peeler. If you are doing the cutting, use a cutting board. Cut away from your body and keep your fingers away from the blade.

That's hot! Be sure an adult is in the kitchen if you use the stove or the oven. Your adult helper can help you cook on the stove and take hot things out of the oven.

Tie it back! If you have long hair, tie it back or wear a hat. If you have long sleeves, roll them up. You want to keep your hair and clothing out of the food and away from flames or other heat sources.

Turn that handle! When cooking on the stove, turn the pot handle toward the back. That way, no one will accidentally bump the pot and knock it off the stove.

Wash it! If you are working with raw eggs or meat, you need to keep things extra clean. After cutting raw meat or fish, wash the knife and the cutting board right away. They must be clean before you use them to cut anything else.

Go slowly! Take your time when you're working. When you are doing something for the first time, such as peeling or grating, be sure not to rush.

Finish the job right!

One of your most important jobs as a chef is to clean up when you're done. Wash the dishes with soap and warm water. Wipe off the countertop or the table. Put away any unused ingredients. The adults in your house will be more excited for you to cook next time if you take charge of cleaning up.

Above all, have fun!

COOKING TOOLS

baking pans

bowls

can opener

colander

cookie sheet

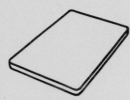
cutting board

dish towel

dry measuring cups

fork

frying pan

grater

knives

large spoon

liquid measuring cup

measuring spoons

oven mitt

plate

saucepans

serrated knife

skewers

spatula

table knife

vegetable peeler

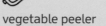
wooden spoon

TECHNIQUES

bake: to cook in the oven

beat: to mix quickly

boil: to heat liquid on a stovetop until it starts to bubble

chop: to cut food into small pieces using a knife

cover: to put a lid on a pan or pot containing food

drain: to pour the liquid off of a food. You can drain food by pouring it into a a colander or strainer. If you are draining water or juice from canned food, you can also use the lid to hold the food back while the liquid pours out.

grate: to use a food grater to shred food into small pieces

grill: to cook on a stove or an outdoor grill

mix: to stir food using a spoon or fork

nonstick: a cooking surface that food is less likely to stick to, such as a nonstick pan

peel: to take off the outer layer

preheat: to turn the oven to the temperature you will need for baking. An oven takes about 15 minutes to heat up.

serrated: a tool, such as a knife, that has a bumpy edge

slice: to cut food into thin pieces

sprinkle: to scatter on top

MEASURING

To measure **dry ingredients**, such as sugar or flour, spoon the ingredient into a measuring cup until it is full. Then use the back of a table knife to level it off. Do not pack it down unless the recipe tells you to. Do not use measuring cups made for liquids.

When you're measuring a **liquid**, such as milk or water, use a clear glass or plastic measuring cup. Set the cup on the table or a counter and pour the liquid into the cup. Pour slowly and stop when the liquid has reached the correct line.

Don't measure your ingredients over the bowl they will go into. If you accidentally spill, you might have way too much!

serves 2

preparation time: 15 minutes
cooking time: 5 minutes

ingredients:
4 large strawberries
½ banana
4 whole wheat freezer waffles
3 tablespoons cream cheese
sprinkle of cinnamon

equipment:
knife
cutting board
toaster or toaster oven
measuring spoons

Waffle Sandwich

Start your day with a delicious waffle sandwich!

1. **Wash** the strawberries under cool water. Use the knife and cutting board to cut off the green strawberry tops. Slice the strawberries into thin slices. (If the pieces of fruit are too big, the sandwich will be too tall—and hard to eat!)

2. **Peel** the banana and **slice** it into thin slices.

3. **Toast** the waffles in the toaster or the toaster oven. They should be a little bit browned.

4. **Spread** half of the cream cheese onto one waffle. Arrange half of the strawberry and banana slices on the cream cheese. **Sprinkle** a little cinnamon on top. **Put** another waffle on top. Repeat to make the second waffle sandwich.

TRY THIS!

Add a sprinkle of coconut on top of the fruit (about 1 teaspoon for each sandwich). You can also use other fruit, such as kiwi, an apple, or pineapple.

serves 2

preparation time: 15 minutes
cooking time: 10 to 20 minutes

ingredients:
about 2 ounces (½ cup)
   Colby-Jack cheese
½ Granny Smith apple
four slices whole wheat bread
1 tablespoon butter, plus more
   for spreading on bread

equipment:
knife
cutting board
large plate (optional)
table knife
frying pan
measuring spoons
spatula (If you're using a
   nonstick pan, be sure the
   spatula is plastic so it
   won't scrape the pan.)

Great Grilled Cheese

There's nothing quite like a hot and tasty grilled cheese sandwich. Try this version with apple in it for a sweet little bit of crunch.

1. Use the knife and the cutting board to **cut** the cheese into ⅛-inch slices.

2. **Wash** the apple under cool water. To cut the apple, first **cut** it in half from top to bottom. Cut one of the halves again from top to bottom. Then cut out and discard the stem and the seeds. Cut into thin slices. Repeat with the other half.

3. **Place** two pieces of bread on a clean work surface. **Place** 4 cheese slices onto each slice so that most of the bread is covered. (The cheese slices don't need to be touching. They will spread out as they melt.)

Turn the page for more Great Grilled Cheese

TRY THIS!
Replace the apple with a slice of **tomato** or some fresh **spinach** leaves.

Great Grilled Cheese continued

4. **Place** apple slices on top of the cheese. **Place** a second piece of bread on top of each sandwich. Use a table knife to spread a thin layer of butter on top of the top slice of bread.

5. Put a frying pan on the stove. Turn on the stove to medium heat. **Place** 1 tablespoon of butter in the pan. Move the butter around with a spatula until it is melted.

6. Get some help to **place** a sandwich, with the buttered side up, into the pan. If your pan is big enough, you can put both sandwiches in the pan.

7. Cook for about 5 minutes. Use a spatula to peek under the bread to see if it is getting brown. If not, check in another minute. The sandwich can burn quickly, so check often. When the first side is browned, slide a spatula under the sandwich and **flip** it over.

8. Cook for another 3 to 5 minutes. When the second side is browned, use the spatula to **remove** the sandwich from the pan. Set it on a plate. Let it cool for 5 minutes. Then **cut** the sandwich in half with the table knife.

9. Cook the other sandwich and serve.

Banana Dog

Invite a friend over for lunch and impress him or her with this unusual sandwich!

1. **Place** a hot dog bun on a plate. **Spread** the peanut butter and the jam or the jelly on the bun with the table knife.

2. **Peel** the bananas and **place** them in the hot dog buns.

3. **Sprinkle** raisins on top. Repeat steps 1 to 3 to make second banana dog.

serves 2

preparation time: 10 to 15 minutes
cooking time: 0 minutes

ingredients:
2 whole wheat hot dog buns
2 tablespoons peanut butter
2 tablespoons jam or jelly (any flavor)
2 ripe bananas
2 tablespoons raisins

equipment:
plate
measuring spoons
table knife

TRY THIS!
You can replace the peanut butter with **cream cheese**, if you like. Or replace the jam or the jelly with **honey**. You can also sprinkle **sunflower seeds** on top for a little extra flavor.

All Wrapped Up

This quick-and-easy sandwich tastes great for lunch or an afternoon snack. Take it in your school lunch for a break from the usual.

serves 2

preparation time: 15 minutes
cooking time: 0 minutes

ingredients:
2 whole wheat tortillas
2 tablespoons cream cheese
4 to 8 deli slices of ham or
    turkey
1 small zucchini
2 pickles

equipment:
knife
cutting board
vegetable peeler
toothpicks

1. **Place** the two tortillas on a clean work surface. **Spread** half of the cream cheese on each tortilla. **Place** 2 to 4 slices of ham or turkey on top of each tortilla. Spread them out around the tortilla.

2. **Wash** the zucchini under cool water. On the cutting board, **cut** off the ends of the zucchini. Then cut the zucchini in half the long way. Use the vegetable peeler to **make** long zucchini strips from the cut side of one of the halves. Place 3 to 4 strips on each tortilla.

3. **Cut** the pickles in half the long way. **Place** the pickles down the middle of the tortilla, end to end, to make one long pickle.

4. **Roll** up each wrap. Set the wrap on the cutting board and cut the wrap into 2-inch sections. Stick a toothpick into each section to hold it together.

TRY THIS!

Try spreading **hummus** on the sandwich instead of cream cheese. You can use strips of **carrots** or **summer squash** instead of **zucchini**. You can also add **avocado** strips, chopped **tomatoes**, **lettuce**, or another favorite sandwich topping to the wrap.

serves 4

preparation time: 20 minutes
cooking time: 20 to 25 minutes

ingredients:

1 large (or 2 small) boneless,
    skinless chicken breast
2 tablespoons vegetable oil
pinch of salt
sprinkle of pepper
1 stalk celery
8 green grapes
¼ cup sunflower seeds
⅓ cup mayonnaise
4 lettuce leaves
8 slices bread

equipment:

baking pan
oven mitts or hot pads
knife
cutting board
medium bowl
measuring cups—¼ cup,
    ⅓ cup
large spoon
clean dish towel or paper
    towels

Chicken Salad Sandwich

Serve this delicious sandwich with some fruit or carrot sticks for a full meal.

1. First, you will cook the chicken. Preheat the oven to 350°F. **Put** the vegetable oil in the baking pan. Take the chicken out of the package. **Rub** both sides of the chicken breast or breasts in the vegetable oil. **Sprinkle** the chicken with several shakes of salt and pepper. (Remember to wash your hands with soap after touching the raw chicken.) Bake for 20 to 25 minutes.

2. To check if the chicken is done, use oven mitts or hot pads to take the baking pan out of the oven. **Cut** near the center of a piece of chicken. If it is still pink in the center, put it back in the oven for another 5 minutes. When the chicken is done, set the baking pan on a hot pad. After the chicken has cooled enough to touch, **cut** the chicken into small pieces using the knife and the cutting board. Set aside. (If you prefer, you can bake the chicken the day before. Keep the cooked chicken in the refrigerator until you are ready to make the salad.)

3. **Wash** the celery and the grapes under cool water. Use the knife and the cutting board to **cut** the grapes in half. Cut the bottom edge off the celery. Cut the rest of the celery in half lengthwise. Then cut it into small pieces.

4. **Place** the chicken, the grapes, and the celery into a medium bowl. **Add** the sunflower seeds and mayonnaise. **Mix** together with a large spoon.

5. **Wash** the lettuce leaves under cool water. Shake the water off the lettuce leaves in the sink. Use a dish towel or paper towels to gently dry the lettuce.

6. **Place** four slices of bread on a clean work surface. **Divide** the salad mixture evenly between the slices of bread. **Add** a lettuce leaf on top. You can fold it in half if it is too large. **Put** another piece of bread on top of each sandwich. **Cut** sandwiches in half.

TRY THIS!

Try adding chopped cashew nuts instead of the sunflower seeds. Or try adding dried cranberries or cherries.

serves 4

preparation time: 20 to 25 minutes
cooking time: 0 minutes

ingredients:

2 slices wheat bread
4 slices cheddar cheese
8 grape tomatoes
½ red pepper
4 lettuce leaves
2 to 3 slices deli turkey
dill pickle slices
4 whole black olives
 (without pits)
mustard (optional)
mayonnaise (optional)

equipment:

knife
cutting board
clean dish towel
4 bamboo skewers

Sandwich on a Stick

Have you ever eaten a sandwich on a stick?
This fancy-looking sandwich is fun to make—and eat!

1. Cut each bread slice using the knife and the cutting board. First cut the bread in half lengthwise. Then cut each half into two equal pieces.

2. Use the knife and the cutting board to **cut** each cheese slice into 1-inch squares.

3. Wash the tomatoes, the red pepper, and the lettuce leaves under cool water. Pat dry with a dish towel. Use the knife and the cutting board to cut the red pepper. **Cut** around the stem of the green pepper. Then cut the pepper in half and remove the seeds. Discard the stem and the seeds. Cut the pepper into 1-inch-wide strips. Then cut the strips into 1-inch squares.

4. **Roll** up the turkey slices. Then **cut** the rolls into 1-inch pieces.

5. Use the skewers to begin making sandwiches. Start with a piece of bread. Then **add** the ingredients you like. To add the turkey, **push** a rolled-up piece onto the skewer. You can **roll** up lettuce and add in the same way. You might add your ingredients in this order: bread, cheese, tomato, lettuce, turkey, tomato, cheese, pickle, pepper, bread, and end with an olive on top.

6. Make all four of the skewer sandwiches. If you like mustard and mayonnaise, put a little glob of each on your plate. Then, if you like, you can dip the sandwich pieces in the mustard and the mayonnaise as you eat.

TRY THIS!

You can add all kinds of extra ingredients to these sandwiches. You might try different **deli meat**, such as **ham** or **sausage**. Or swap in different vegetables or fruits such as **green peppers**, **mushrooms**, **grapes**, or **apples**. Use your imagination!

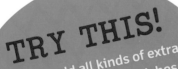

serves 6

preparation time: 15 to
20 minutes
cooking time: 25 to 30 minutes

ingredients:

1 medium onion
1 large carrot
1 14-ounce can diced tomatoes
1 6-ounce can tomato paste
1 pound ground turkey
2 tablespoons vegetable oil
2 teaspoons Worcestershire
  sauce
1 teaspoon brown sugar
½ teaspoon salt
¼ teaspoon black pepper
6 whole wheat hamburger buns

equipment:

knife
cutting board
grater
can opener
large frying pan
spatula
measuring spoons

Turkey Sloppy Joe

There's nothing like a satisfying sloppy joe when you're hungry!

1. **Cut** off both ends of the onion. Set the onion on one of the flat parts you made by cutting it. Cut the onion in half. **Peel** off and discard the papery layers around the outside. Lay the onion half flat on the cutting board. **Cut** the onion crosswise into semicircular slices. Then **chop** the slices into small pieces. Repeat with the other half. Set aside.

2. **Wash** the carrot under cool water. **Grate** the carrot using the grater. You should have about ½ cup. Discard the carrot stems. Set aside the grated carrot.

3. **Open** the diced tomato and tomato paste cans with a can opener. Set aside. **Open** the turkey package so it will be ready to use. (Remember to wash your hands with soap after touching the raw turkey.)

4. **Place** a frying pan on the stove. **Put** the oil in the pan and turn the heat to high. Place the onions in the pan. Cook for 5 minutes, **stirring** occasionally with a spatula. **Add** the carrot. Cook for 3 more minutes.

5. Add the turkey to the pan. Break it up with the spatula and **stir**. Cook the meat about 10 to 12 minutes, until it is all brown. When it is done, there should be no parts that are still pink.

6. Add the diced tomatoes and their juice, the tomato paste, the Worcestershire sauce, the brown sugar, salt, and pepper. **Stir** well. Turn down the heat to low and cook for 10 minutes.

7. Serve the sloppy joes in hamburger buns.

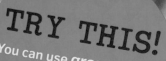

TRY THIS!
You can use **ground beef** instead of turkey in this recipe.

serves 4

preparation time: 15 minutes
cooking time: 10 minutes

ingredients:
4 lettuce leaves
1 medium onion
1 egg
½ cup frozen corn
1 15-ounce can black beans
½ cup bread crumbs
1 teaspoon chili powder
1 teaspoon cumin
½ teaspoon salt
2 tablespoons vegetable oil
4 hamburger buns
ketchup or mustard

equipment:
clean dish towel or paper
   towels
knife
cutting board
small bowl
fork
can opener
colander
large bowl
½ cup measuring cup
measuring spoons
frying pan (a nonstick pan
   works well)
spatula

Black Bean Veggie Burger

This hearty, healthy veggie burger tastes great!

1. **Wash** the lettuce leaves. Pat dry with a dish towel or paper towels. Set aside.

2. **Cut** off both ends of the onion. Set the onion on one of the flat parts you made by cutting it. Cut the onion in half. **Peel** off and discard the papery layers around the outside. Lay the onion half flat on the cutting board. **Cut** the onion crosswise into semicircular slices. Then **chop** the slices into small pieces. Repeat with the other half. Set aside.

3. Crack the egg into a small bowl. **Beat** lightly with a fork. Set aside.

4. Measure the corn and place it in a microwave-safe bowl. **Heat** the corn for 1 minute, or until it is not frozen.

5. Use the can opener to **open** the beans. Put a colander in the sink and **pour** the beans into the colander to drain the liquid. Then **pour** the beans into a large bowl. **Mash** well with a fork.

Turn the page for more Black Bean Veggie Burger

TRY THIS!
You can add many yummy toppings to your burger. Try sliced cheese, avocado, or tomato.

Black Bean Veggie Burger continued

6. Add the onion, the egg, the corn, the bread crumbs, the chili powder, cumin, and salt to the beans. **Mix** well.

7. Use your hands to form the mixture into four patties. Wash your hands after making the patties.

8. Place a large frying pan on the stove. **Put** the oil in the pan and stir to coat the pan with the oil. Turn the burner under the pan to medium. Wait about 2 minutes. Use a spatula to **place** the patties in the pan. Cook about 4 minutes, or until they are brown on the bottom. Use a spatula to **flip** the burgers over. Then cook for 4 more minutes.

9. Serve in the hamburger buns with the lettuce on top and ketchup or mustard.

Inside-Out Sandwich

This sandwich has peanuty noodles inside. And instead of bread, it uses lettuce as a wrapper.

1. **Add** water to a saucepan, **cover**, and place on the stove. Turn the burner under the pot on high. Heat until water boils. **Add** spaghetti, stirring with a wooden spoon until it is all under water. Cook for 8 to 10 minutes, or follow the directions on the box. When it is done, ask an adult to **drain** the pasta into a colander in the sink. Run cool water over the spaghetti.

Turn the page for more Inside-Out Sandwich

serves 4 to 6

cooking time: 15 minutes
preparation time: 15 minutes

ingredients:
6 cups water
8 ounces spaghetti
1 cucumber
4 to 8 lettuce leaves
¼ cup peanut butter
2 tablespoons soy sauce
1 tablespoon vegetable oil
½ teaspoon ground ginger
2 teaspoons brown sugar

equipment:
liquid measuring cup
large saucepan with lid
wooden spoon
colander
clean dish towel or
paper towels
vegetable peeler
knife
cutting board
medium
bowl

spoon
measuring
spoons
measuring cups—
1 cup, ¼ cup
large bowl
4 to 6 plates for serving

Inside-Out Sandwich continued

2. **Wash** the cucumber and the lettuce under cool water. Dry the lettuce with a dish towel or paper towels. To cut the cucumber, first, **peel** it with a vegetable peeler. Then use the knife to **cut** off the ends and discard them. Cut the cucumber in slices. Then **chop** the slices into smaller pieces. Set aside.

3. **Place** the peanut butter, soy sauce, vegetable oil, ginger, and brown sugar in a medium bowl. **Mix** together well with a spoon.

4. **Put** the spaghetti into a large bowl. Then **add** the cucumber and the sauce. **Mix** well.

5. **Put** a lettuce leaf on a plate. **Spoon** some of the spaghetti mixture onto the lettuce. **Roll** the lettuce up, folding the edges. Pick up the lettuce sandwich with your hands to eat it. Watch out, this one can get messy!

TRY THIS!

Add ¼ cup of chopped **red pepper** when you add the **cucumber**. Or try adding 2 **green onions**, chopped into small pieces. If you like spicy food, you can add a sprinkle of **cayenne pepper**. Add just a tiny sprinkle at a time. Then mix it in and taste it to see if it is spicy enough. If you add too much, it might be too spicy to eat!

serves 4

preparation time: 15 to
20 minutes
cooking time: 1 minute

ingredients:
¼ green pepper
2 green onions
½ medium tomato
½ cup frozen corn
1 15-ounce can black beans
1 tablespoon taco seasoning
4 halves whole wheat pita
   bread

equipment:
serrated knife
cutting board
measuring cups—½ cup,
   ¼ cup
microwave-safe bowl
can opener
colander
large bowl
measuring spoons
spoon

Pita Pocket

This sandwich in a pocket will fill you up
when you're hungry. This would make a
great sandwich for a school lunch.

1. Wash the green pepper, the green onions, and
the tomato under cool water. Use the knife and
the cutting board to cut the pepper. **Cut** around
the stem of the green pepper. Then cut
the green pepper in half and
remove the seeds. Discard
the stem and the seeds.
Chop the rest of the
green pepper. Set aside.

2. Use a knife and a cutting board to cut the green
onions. **Cut** off the roots and discard. Remove
any dry or wilted green parts. Then **slice** the
onions into small pieces about
½-inch long. You can use
both the white and green
parts of the onion.

3. Use the knife and cutting board to cut the tomato. It works best to cut a tomato with a serrated knife, a knife with bumps along the sharp edge. To cut the tomato, first cut out the brown or green circle on the top. Discard it. Then **chop** the rest of the tomato.

Turn the page for more Pita Pocket

TRY THIS!
You can add chopped **avocado** or **olives** to the mix. Or try adding some **lettuce** to the pita bread before spooning in the bean mixture. You could also roll this sandwich up in a tortilla instead of using pita bread.

4. Measure the corn and place it in the microwave-safe bowl. **Heat** the corn for 1 minute, or until it is not frozen.

5. Use the can opener to **open** the beans. Put a colander in the sink and **pour** the beans into the colander to drain the liquid.

6. **Put** the beans in the large bowl.

7. **Add** the green pepper, the green onions, the tomatoes, and the corn to the bowl. **Add** the taco seasoning. Mix together with a spoon.

8. If the pita bread you are using is not **cut** in half, use a knife and a cutting board to cut it in half. Carefully **open** each pita bread half so it makes a pocket. Use the spoon to **divide** the veggie mixture among the 4 pita halves.

SPECIAL INGREDIENTS

bamboo skewer: a stick made out of bamboo and used to put food on. These skewers are often used to grill food outside and may be found with the grilling items in a grocery store.

bread crumbs: dried bread crumbs, which you can find in the baking or bread aisle at the grocery store

cashew nuts: the nuts of the cashew tree. Look for them in the bulk section or snack food aisle at the grocery store.

chili powder: a blend of dried, ground spices, often used to flavor chili. Look for it in the dried spice and herb section of your grocery store.

Colby-Jack cheese: cheese made from Colby and Monterey Jack cheeses

cumin: a ground spice that is used to flavor many Mexican and Indian dishes. Look for it in the dried spice and herb section of the grocery store.

Granny Smith apple: a type of apple that has green skin when ripe

grape tomatoes: small tomatoes shaped like grapes. They are found in the produce section of a grocery store. You can also use cherry tomatoes.

ground ginger: a spice made of ginger root, found with the spices in the grocery store

pita bread: a flat bread with a pocket inside, often used in Middle Eastern cooking. Look for pita bread in the deli section of most large grocery stores.

soy sauce: a salty sauce often used in Chinese and Japanese dishes. Look for it in the ethnic foods section of most grocery stores.

taco seasoning: a packet of seasonings for tacos, which can be found in the baking and spices aisle or with the Mexican foods in the grocery store

tomato paste: a thick paste made from cooked, pureed tomatoes. Look for it with other canned foods in the grocery store.

Worcestershire sauce: a sauce often used when cooking meat

zucchini: a skinny, green vegetable that grows on a vine. Look for it in the produce section or at a farmers' market.

FURTHER READING AND WEBSITES

ChooseMyPlate.gov
http://www.choosemyplate.gov
/children-over-five.html
Download coloring pages, play an
interactive computer game, and get
lots of nutrition information at this U.S.
Department of Agriculture website.

**Cleary, Brian P. Food Is CATegorical
series.** Minneapolis: Millbrook Press, 2011.
This seven-book illustrated series offers
a fun introduction to the food groups and
other important health information.

Fizzy's Lunch Lab
http://pbskids.org/lunchlab/#
Check out fun games, videos, quizzes, and
recipes at this site.

Lord, John Vernon, and Janet Burroway, *The
Giant Jam Sandwich*, New York: Houghton
Mifflin Harcourt, 1972.
A jam sandwich saves the day in this story
about a town overrun with wasps.

Sandwiches, Burgers & Wraps
http://spoonful.com/recipes
/sandwiches-burgers-wraps-gallery
This website has many fun recipes written
just for kids.

INDEX